UQAI in Remote Work

The New Reality Balancing Productivity and Well-being

KATIA DORIA DA FONSECA DOS SANTOS
31/1/2023

Dedication:

To my beloved children, Mario (Teik), Bruna, Victor, and Bárbara, who are the inspiration and reason for my relentless pursuit of knowledge. You are my strength and motivation to share my ideas and experiences.

To my husband, José de Vasconcelos Filho, whose collaboration and support were instrumental in the creation of this book. Your unwavering dedication and support are a precious gift in my life.

To my dear grandchildren, Davi, Vivi, and João Gabriel, who represent the continuity of our stories and the hope for a bright future. May this book inspire you to explore your passions and seek truth in all things.

To my sons-in-law and daughters-in-law, Nikolas Bucvar, Eduardo, Jana, and Jacque, who strengthen our family with their love, support, and valuable contributions. I am grateful for being part of this journey and for sharing your perspectives and enriching experiences.

May this be dedicated to all of you, my beloved family, with all my love and gratitude.

Katia Doria da Fonseca Vasconcelos

INTRODUCTION

In today's world, Remote work has become a common reality and a fundamental aspect of professional dynamics. With the increasing adoption of technologies and the pursuit of flexibility, companies and professionals are exploring new ways of working, regardless of their physical location. However, this new scenario brings unique challenges, such as the need to balance productivity and employee well-being.

To tackle these challenges and ensure a healthy and efficient

Remote work environment, it is essential to adopt an approach that goes beyond technical skills and considers emotional, behavioral, and adaptive aspects. In this context, the USIQ (Universal Synchronous Intelligence Quotient) emerges as a comprehensive and powerful metric.

In this book, titled "UQAI no Remote Work: The New Reality Balancing Productivity and Well-being," we will explore the importance of USIQ as an artificial intelligence tool in the context of Remote work. UQAI (Advanced Universal Synchronous Intelligence

Quotient) is an evolution of the UQ concept, empowered by technology, that allows for a deeper and more accurate analysis of key aspects of Remote work.

Throughout the following pages, we will delve into the definition and scientific foundation of UQAI, highlighting its ability to measure not only task efficiency but also aspects such as resilience, adaptability, synchronicity, and emotional control. We will explore how UQAI can be incorporated within companies and used as an assessment and continuous development tool for remote employees.

Furthermore, we will address the importance of establishing clear protocols and guidelines for UQAI implementation, ensuring consistent and unbiased evaluations. We will discuss the benefits and challenges associated with using UQAI, providing practical guidance for its effective application in the context of Remote work.

By the end of this book, we hope you will grasp the potential of UQAI as a powerful tool to promote the balance between productivity and well-being in

Remote work. Through the conscious and strategic use of UQAI, companies will be able to make informed decisions, develop essential skills in employees, and build a more productive and healthy Remote work environment.

We invite you to embark on this journey of discovery and deepening, exploring the potential of UQAI and its practical application in the new reality of Remote work. Together, we will be prepared to face the challenges and make the most of the opportunities that this transformation offers us.

TABLE OF CONTENTS

UQ DEFINITION: UNIVERSAL SYNCHRONOUS
INTELLIGENCE QUOTIENT

The UQ (Universal Synchronous Intelligence Quotient) is a powerful concept that seeks to understand and balance essential human potentials. It encompasses different dimensions, including 360-degree vision, resilience, adaptability, synchronicity, and emotional control.

UQ can be defined as a metric and parameter that allow us to objectively measure and evaluate human potentials over time and among individuals. It provides a clear view of where we stand in relation to the balance of these potentials and identifies areas that need to be developed to achieve a more effective equilibrium.

Determining UQ involves evaluating each of the aforementioned dimensions. Each dimension is scored based on a specific scale, reflecting the level of development or skill in each area. These scores are then combined to calculate an individual's total UQ.

As a metric, UQ provides us with a reference criterion, a benchmark, or a threshold for assessing the balance of potentials. It helps us determine if we are achieving an appropriate equilibrium in each of the evaluated dimensions. Based on this parameter, we can devise strategies and enhancements to achieve a more effective balance.

UQ goes beyond a simple assessment as it aims to promote continuous and purposeful development of human potentials. It offers a roadmap for maximizing human potential, driving personal and professional excellence.

By understanding and applying UQ, we can achieve exceptional results, creating a new reality based on the balance of human potentials. This approach provides a solid foundation for success and well-being, enabling us to unleash our full potential and face challenges with confidence and effectiveness.

UQ is a revolutionary approach that redefines how we

understand and value human potentials. By incorporating UQ into our life and work, we can unlock a new level of performance, satisfaction, and fulfillment.

THE SCIENTIFIC FOUNDATION OF UQ

The theory of UQ (Universal Synchronous Intelligence Quotient) is supported by a solid scientific foundation, backed by research and studies conducted by renowned experts in various fields. Several authors and their research have contributed to the substantiation of this theory. Below are some relevant examples:

1. Daniel Goleman: Author of the book "Emotional Intelligence," Goleman is a reference in the field of emotional intelligence. His research demonstrates how emotional balance is crucial for personal and professional success. The theory of UQ incorporates

the importance of emotional control as one of the essential aspects for the balance of human potentials.

2. Clayton Christensen: Professor at Harvard Business School, Christensen is known for his work on disruptive innovation. He highlights the need for adaptability and paradigm shifts to achieve success in business. UQ addresses adaptability as one of the potentials to be balanced, taking into account the challenges of Remote work.

3. Carol Dweck: Psychologist and author of the book "Mindset," Dweck

emphasizes the importance of a growth mindset in achieving success. The theory of UQ aligns with this concept, encouraging continuous development of human potentials through balance and personal growth.

4. Daniel Kahneman: Nobel laureate economist and psychologist, Kahneman is known for his research on human behavior and decision-making. His contribution to UQ relates to the importance of a positive perspective and the ability to approach challenges as opportunities for learning.

These are just a few examples of the many researchers and authors whose works support the theory of UQ. Their research and studies provide scientific evidence that underpins the importance of balancing human potentials for success and well-being. By integrating this knowledge, UQ offers a comprehensive and evidence-based approach to achieving effective balance in different areas of life.

UQ AS A PARAMETER AND METRIC: AN
APPROACH FOR POTENTIAL EVALUATION

UQ (Universal Qualification) is a widely adopted methodology by organizations as a parameter and metric for evaluating the individual potentials of their employees. This holistic approach takes into consideration fundamental aspects such as 360-degree vision, resilience, adaptability, synchronicity, and emotional control.

When used as a parameter, UQ establishes a set of criteria that define the minimum level of potentials employees should reach to achieve specific objectives or company requirements. These criteria can be tailored to the specific needs of each role or position.

By using UQ as a metric, it becomes possible to quantify and measure employees' performance in relation to the evaluated potentials. Each aspect of UQ is assigned a specific score, and the sum of these scores results in a value that reflects the level of individual potential development.

By employing UQ as a parameter and metric, organizations have the opportunity to objectively and consistently assess their employees' potentials. This provides a solid foundation for decision-making related to promotions, career development, training programs, and other initiatives aimed at individual and organizational growth.

Furthermore, UQ as a parameter and metric promotes a culture of self-improvement and continuous enhancement. Employees are encouraged to seek the advancement of their potentials, as they have a clear reference to the established criteria and scores.

It is important to note that UQ as a parameter and metric should not be used in isolation but integrated into a broader people management system, considering other relevant aspects such as technical competencies, professional experience, and organizational values.

In summary, UQ as a parameter and metric offers organizations a structured and objective approach to evaluate and develop employees' potentials. By establishing clear and measurable criteria, it provides a solid basis for decision-making regarding individual and organizational development, becoming a powerful tool in the pursuit of excellence and sustainable growth for companies.

THE APPLICABILITY OF UQ (UNIVERSAL SYNCHRONOUS INTELLIGENCE QUOTIENT)

The applicability of UQ (Universal Synchronous Intelligence Quotient) encompasses various areas of life, including work, relationships, and personal development. Through understanding and applying UQ, we can achieve effective balance of human potentials, driving positive outcomes and greater well-being.

In the context of work, UQ can be applied to enhance productivity, creativity, and adaptability of individuals and teams. By assessing and developing potentials related to 360-degree vision, resilience, adaptability, synchronicity, and emotional control, we can enhance the skills necessary to effectively navigate workplace challenges.

Furthermore, UQ is relevant in interpersonal relationships, enabling more effective communication, empathy, and collaboration. The balance of human potentials promoted by UQ contributes to building healthy, respectful, and productive relationships, both in the workplace and personal life.

In the realm of personal development, UQ provides a framework for self-assessment and continuous growth. By understanding our potentials and identifying areas that require development, we can devise strategies to improve and maximize our performance across all dimensions of UQ. This allows us to achieve a higher level of satisfaction and personal fulfillment, driving our growth and development.

The application of UQ involves the use of tools such as questionnaires and quizzes that help us objectively measure and assess human potentials. These tools provide valuable insights into our current balance and guide the necessary development to achieve a more effective equilibrium.

It is important to note that the applicability of UQ requires a continuous and personalized approach. As we develop and face new challenges, adjustments need to be made to maintain the balance of potentials over time. In doing so, we can achieve lasting results and enjoy a more satisfying and fulfilled life, both personally and professionally.

PRACTICAL EXAMPLES OF UNIVERSAL SYNCHRONOUS INTELLIGENCE QUOTIENT (UQ) APPLICATION

Practical examples of how the Universal Synchronous Intelligence Quotient (UQ) can be applied in different contexts:

1. UQ in the workplace: Imagine a company that wants to assess the balance of human potentials among its employees to promote a more productive and healthy work environment. Through questionnaires and UQ-based analysis tools, the company can gather information about employees' 360-degree vision, resilience, adaptability, synchronicity, and emotional control. Based on the results, areas for development can be

identified, and strategies can be devised to improve the balance of these potentials.

2. UQ in education: In an educational institution, educators can use UQ to assess students' development in various areas beyond academic performance. Through tailored questionnaires, students can provide information about their comprehensive learning perspective, ability to handle challenges, adaptability, collaboration, and emotional control. These data help educators personalize their teaching approach and provide appropriate support for each student.

3. UQ in leadership: A leader can use UQ to evaluate their own leadership capacity and balance their potentials to promote a more effective work environment. Through self-assessment and feedback from team members, the leader can identify strengths and weaknesses in relation to 360-degree vision, resilience, adaptability, synchronicity, and emotional control. This allows the leader to develop strategies for personal improvement and adopt a more balanced and effective approach in guiding their team.

These are just a few examples of how UQ can be applied in practice. The methodology of questionnaires and continuous analysis enables individuals and organizations to identify areas for development and work towards a more effective balance. By incorporating the principles of UQ in different areas of life, it is possible to enhance human potential and achieve exceptional results.

Example of UQ Application:

Preparing Thomas for Remote work: Let's imagine the case of Thomas, a professional seeking a Remote work opportunity. Here's a basic example of an assessment protocol for the evaluator: Company X: Protocol

01/01 UQ Authentication for Remote work Instructions to the Evaluator:

1. Minimum Accepted Percentage for Remote work: The minimum accepted percentage for granting Remote work permission is 89% of the total UQ.
2. Evaluation Calculation Instructions: Use the UQ questionnaire filled out by the candidate to assign an individual score for each evaluated aspect: 360-degree vision, resilience, adaptability, synchronicity, and emotional control. Sum all the scores to obtain the candidate's total UQ.

3. Training Referral Instructions: If the candidate does not meet the minimum accepted percentage for Remote work or the minimum requirement of 3 points in emotional control potential, refer them to specific training for developing the potentials that need improvement.

4. Remote work Approval Instructions: If the candidate achieves the minimum accepted percentage for Remote work and meets all established requirements, they are approved for Remote work. Otherwise, the candidate will only be recommended for on-site work.

This is an example of a UQ authentication protocol for Remote work, which establishes guidelines and criteria for assessing and granting Remote work permission based on the candidate's total UQ. The protocol aims to ensure that candidates achieve an adequate balance in their potentials and are prepared to face the challenges and demands of Remote work.

Here's a basic example of Remote work Evaluation:

UQ EVALUATION QUIZ DEVELOPED FOR Thomas:

1. 360-degree vision: a) Yes, I have a clear vision from all angles of my Remote work.

(Score: 3 points) b) I sometimes struggle to have a complete understanding of how my Remote work is organized. (Score: 2 points) c) I find it difficult to visualize all perspectives of my Remote work. (Score: 1 point)

2. Resilience: a) I can handle adversity and maintain good emotional balance in Remote work. (Score: 3 points) b) Sometimes, I have difficulty dealing with adversity, and it affects my productivity. (Score: 2 points) c) I struggle to recover from adverse situations, which negatively impacts my performance. (Score: 1 point)

3. Adaptability: a) I can easily adapt to new circumstances and demands in Remote work. (Score: 3 points) b) I need some time to adjust to changes, but I can adapt. (Score: 2 points) c) I have difficulty adapting to changes, which affects my performance in Remote work. (Score: 1 point)

4. Synchronicity: a) I can maintain a harmonious and coordinated workflow in the Remote work environment. (Score: 3 points) b) Sometimes, I struggle to synchronize my tasks and deadlines in Remote work. (Score: 2 points) c) I have difficulty maintaining efficient

synchronicity in my Remote work. (Score: 1 point)
5. Emotional Control: a) I can maintain emotional control and deal with the pressures and stresses of Remote work. (Score: 3 points) b) In some situations, I lose a bit of emotional control, but I can quickly recover. (Score: 2 points) c) I have difficulty controlling my emotions, and it affects my productivity in Remote work. (Score: 1 point)

Simulated Score Corresponding to Thomas's Answers:

Thomas responded:

1. Answer: a (360-degree vision)

2. Answer: b (Resilience)
3. Answer: c (Adaptability)
4. Answer: a (Synchronicity)
5. Answer: b (Emotional Control)

After Thomas completes the UQ quiz, we will calculate the score obtained in each evaluated aspect. The score will be assigned based on Thomas's responses. Here is the calculation:

360-degree vision: Obtained score - 3 points Resilience: Obtained score - 2 points Adaptability: Obtained score - 1 point Synchronicity: Obtained score - 3 points Emotional Control: Obtained score - 2 points

Now, let's sum all the scores to obtain Thomas's total UQ: Total UQ = 360-degree vision + Resilience + Adaptability + Synchronicity + Emotional Control = 3 + 2 + 1 + 3 + 2 = 11 points

With a score of 11 points, let's calculate the percentage in relation to the desired UQ. If the desired UQ is 15 (100%), we can calculate the percentage as follows:

Obtained UQ Percentage = (Obtained UQ / Desired UQ) * 100 = (11 / 15) * 100 = 73.33%

Therefore, Thomas obtained a score of 73.33% in relation to the desired UQ.

According to the established protocol, the minimum accepted percentage for Remote work is 89%. As Thomas did not meet this requirement, the evaluator will provide feedback indicating that he is not currently eligible for Remote work.

In this feedback, the evaluator will highlight the areas where Thomas performed well, such as 360-degree vision and synchronicity, as well as areas where he needs improvement, such as resilience, adaptability, and emotional control. Specific recommendations will be provided for the development of these potentials through training and strategies, aiming to prepare

Thomas for future Remote work opportunities.

The evaluator's analysis and recommendations will be crucial for Thomas to direct his development efforts, enhance his potentials, and strive to achieve the minimum required score for Remote work in the future.

UQAI: EMPOWERING UQ WITH ARTIFICIAL INTELLIGENCE

In the previous chapter, we explored the concept of Universal Synchronous Intelligence Quotient (UQ) as a comprehensive metric for assessing performance in Remote work. Now, we are taking it to a new level by introducing UQAI (Amplified Universal Synchronous Intelligence Quotient), an advanced tool that enhances UQ with the use of Artificial Intelligence (AI).

Artificial Intelligence has revolutionized various sectors, and the Remote work environment is no exception. With UQAI, it is possible to elevate the assessment and analysis of UQ aspects to a more sophisticated and accurate level. AI enables the tool to track and evaluate different elements of UQ simultaneously, from both the company's and remote employees' perspectives.

UQAI functions as an intelligent virtual assistant, capable of analyzing real-time data, identifying patterns, and providing valuable insights to enhance performance in Remote work. With its processing and learning capabilities, UQAI can help identify areas of opportunity, points for improvement, and strategies to optimize productivity and well-being in the remote environment.

One of the great advantages of UQAI is its customization

capability. The tool can adapt to individual preferences and needs of employees, providing personalized recommendations to increase efficiency and satisfaction in Remote work. This creates a more personalized and tailored experience, taking into account the characteristics and peculiarities of each professional.

Furthermore, UQAI can automate repetitive and routine tasks, freeing up employees to focus on higher-value activities. AI can take on operational tasks such as scheduling meetings, email screening, and document organization, allowing employees to direct their energy toward more strategic and creative projects.

However, when using UQAI, it is important to also consider the challenges and ethical issues involved in the use of Artificial Intelligence. Ensuring the protection of employees' privacy, data security, and transparency in the decisions made by UQAI is crucial. Responsible and ethical implementation is essential to gain the trust and respect of employees.

In summary, UQAI represents a significant advancement in using UQ as a metric in Remote work. With the aid of Artificial Intelligence, it is possible to amplify and enhance performance assessment, providing a deeper and more comprehensive view of UQ aspects. UQAI offers benefits such as customization, automation, and valuable insights to optimize productivity and well-being in the remote environment.

At the end of this chapter, we invite readers to reflect on the possibilities and impacts of UQAI in Remote work. We will delve deeper into success stories, practical examples, and additional considerations regarding the implementation of this tool. Get ready to embark on a journey of discovery and learning, uncovering the potential of UQAI to drive the new reality of Remote work.

REMOTE WORK IN THE CURRENT ERA: UNVEILING THE PRINCIPLES OF UQ PARAMETERIZATION

Remote work has become an increasingly widespread practice in today's professional landscape, offering numerous benefits for both companies and employees. However, despite this growing adoption, we are still in the early stages of fully exploring the potential of these benefits and face significant challenges when implementing remote service delivery. Let's now examine, in more depth, some relevant aspects from the perspectives of companies and remote employees.

Profile of Companies Utilizing Remote Employees:

1. Challenges related to 360-degree vision: • Excessive or lack of communication in

interpersonal relationships, hindering expectation alignment and effective collaboration. • Decision-making without accurate data, impairing effectiveness and assertiveness in strategic choices. • Difficulty in meeting established timelines, affecting organization and project progress. • Failures in conventional vertical leadership that does not adapt to the challenges and dynamics of Remote work. • Impact on problem-solving, with the lack of face-to-face interaction and delays in resolving critical issues. • Overestimation of expectations due to a lack of comprehensive vision of Remote work demands and peculiarities.

2. Challenges related to Resilience: • Unreliable dependability in both delivering results and maintaining strong professional relationships. • Limited flexibility, hindering adaptation to sudden changes and the needs of Remote work. • Absence or lack of understanding of social support, impeding the sense of belonging and support in the Remote work environment. • Inadequate emotional management, with difficulties in handling stress, pressure, and emotions arising from

Remote work. • Overly optimistic or pessimistic perspectives, impacting the ability to objectively assess situations and make balanced decisions. • Importance of self-care for the physical and mental well-being of remote employees.

3. Challenges related to Adaptability: • Resistance to change, hindering the incorporation of new processes, tools, and technologies necessary for efficient Remote work. • Difficulty in adjusting to different demands and projects, requiring flexibility and adaptive skills. • Limitations in quickly

adapting to changes in the Remote work environment and team dynamics.

4. Challenges related to Synchronicity: • Difficulty in maintaining efficient communication and coordination among remote teams due to the lack of face-to-face contact. • Challenges in synchronizing schedules and availability for collaboration, considering different time zones and individual needs. • Difficulty in synchronizing tasks and deadlines in a distributed work environment, requiring effective time and priority management.

5. Challenges related to Emotional Control: • Stress and emotional overload resulting from the pressure and demands of Remote work, requiring strategies for emotional balance. • Difficulty in dealing with emotions arising from Remote work, such as loneliness, anxiety, and frustration. • Importance of adopting emotional control practices and techniques to ensure well-being and productivity in the remote environment.

By understanding these specific challenges faced by companies and employees in Remote work, we can seek appropriate solutions and strategies to overcome them. The Universal Synchronous Intelligence Quotient (UQ) can play a fundamental role in this process, offering a comprehensive and parameterized approach to enhance discipline, performance, and balance in Remote work.

Profile of Employees Utilizing Remote work:

Challenges

360-degree vision: • Difficulty in maintaining effective communication with the team and leaders due to physical distance. • Limitations in obtaining accurate and up-to-date information to make informed decisions. • Challenges in meeting established deadlines and timelines without in-person supervision. • Need for self-management and independence in Remote work. • Overload of issues and challenges that need to be individually resolved. • Misaligned or unclear expectations due to a lack of comprehensive company vision.

Resilience: • Need to maintain high reliability and consistency in delivering results. • Flexibility to handle unexpected changes and quickly adapt to new situations. • Seeking social support and connections with coworkers in a remote environment. • Ability to manage emotions and cope with stress and pressure in Remote work. • Adopting a balanced and realistic perspective, avoiding extreme optimism or pessimism. • Practicing self-care to ensure physical and mental well-being.

Adaptability: • Openness and willingness to learn new tools, processes, and technologies. • Ability to adjust to different demands and projects, prioritizing tasks and adapting to different Remote work environments. • Flexibility to deal with changes in Remote work strategies and directions.

Synchronicity: • Effective communication skills in a virtual environment, ensuring productive collaboration. • Availability to synchronize schedules with the team, considering time zones and individual needs. • Ability to coordinate tasks and deadlines in a distributed work environment with different geographic locations.

Emotional Control: • Managing stress and emotions related to Remote work. • Adopting strategies to maintain emotional balance in a remote environment. • Focusing on well-being and mental health, avoiding burnout and exhaustion.

By understanding the specific challenges faced by employees in Remote work, it is possible to develop strategies and solutions to support their performance and well-being. The Universal Synchronous Intelligence Quotient (UQ) can be a valuable tool for assessing and developing the necessary skills to address these challenges and achieve a healthy balance in Remote work.

Remember that UQ offers a parameterized and comprehensive approach, allowing both companies and employees to identify areas for improvement and adopt practices that maximize the potential of Remote work. The parameterization of UQ as an artificial intelligence tool, UQAI, provides a comprehensive solution to tackle the challenges of Remote work. Customized to meet the specific needs of each company and industry, UQAI is integrated into the work environment, enabling continuous and simultaneous monitoring of various aspects related to employee performance and well-being.

With UQAI, it is possible to accurately identify areas that require attention, such as 360-degree vision, adaptability, synchronicity, resilience, and emotional control. This artificial intelligence tool allows for in-depth analysis of each of these elements, providing valuable insights and guiding specific actions to promote significant improvements.

By following an established protocol based on the information collected and analyzed by UQAI, companies and employees can benefit from a structured and goal-oriented approach to maximize their potential in Remote work. UQAI provides personalized recommendations, suggesting strategies to strengthen communication and collaboration, overcome obstacles related to adapting to changes, optimize task and deadline synchronization, manage emotional pressure, and maintain a healthy balance in the Remote work environment.

In this way, UQAI presents itself as a powerful artificial intelligence tool capable of boosting productivity, well-being, and efficiency in Remote work. By utilizing the parameterization of UQ through UQAI, companies and employees can overcome the inherent challenges of Remote work and make the most of the benefits this mode of service delivery offers.

Human success is driven by the balance of UQ (Universal Synchronous Intelligence Quotient), a concept supported by scientific research and case studies. Several studies have explored the aspects of UQ and its effects in different areas of human life.

A study conducted by researchers from Stanford University revealed the importance of developing resilience and emotional control in achieving positive outcomes in careers and relationships. This research demonstrated how the ability to deal with adversity and control emotions contributes to making informed decisions and building healthy and productive relationships.

Clayton Christensen, renowned professor of Business Administration at Harvard, highlights that disruptive innovation requires a change in approach and overcoming outdated paradigms. He emphasizes that success lies in embracing change and quickly adapting to new circumstances.

Daniel Kahneman, psychologist and Nobel laureate economist, reminds us that our decisions are influenced by how we frame problems. By adopting a positive perspective and viewing challenges as learning opportunities, we can make more informed decisions and achieve superior results. The theory of emotional intelligence, developed by Daniel Goleman, also aligns with the concept of UQ, emphasizing the importance of emotional balance for personal and professional success.

Howard Gardner, renowned psychologist and professor at the Harvard Graduate School of Education, emphasizes the importance of balancing and developing all our intelligences. He encourages us to reprogram our educational approach, valuing not only logical-mathematical intelligence but also emotional, musical, spatial, and other intelligences, allowing us to explore our full potential.

These prominent figures, along with other advocates of innovative thinking, reinforce the importance of adopting a new perspective when facing problems. By balancing our potentials through 360-degree vision, resilience, adaptability, synchronicity, and emotional control, we will be prepared to tackle challenges with confidence, creativity, and effectiveness. This approach also relates to other relevant theories and concepts, such as Carol Dweck's growth mindset, which highlights the importance of a growth-oriented mindset in pursuing success.

In this book, we have extensively explored the principles of UQ and how they relate to different areas of human life. We have examined scientific research, inspiring case studies, and relevant theories to provide a broad and well-founded insight into the balance of UQ and its impact on personal and professional success.

Throughout the chapters, we delved into the concept of UQ alongside Artificial Intelligence (AI) and how this powerful partnership can drive success in all areas of life.

In the first chapter, we explored in detail the concept of UQ and its fundamental role in human balance and development. We saw how UQ is based on scientific research and case studies that prove its relevance in the pursuit of success. UQ allows us to understand and balance our potentials, including 360-degree vision, adaptability, resilience, synchronicity, and emotional control.

Next, we delved into the fascinating world of Artificial Intelligence, understanding its foundations and applications. We explored how AI can process vast amounts of data, identify patterns, and perform complex analyses, providing valuable insights in various areas of life.

Finally, we united these two powerful concepts: UQ and AI. We analyzed how the collaboration between UQ and AI can drive success in professional life, strengthen interpersonal relationships, transform education, simplify daily life, and promote balanced health. We saw practical examples of how AI can amplify our UQ potentials, providing innovative solutions and enhancing our ability to face challenges.

Throughout this book, you have discovered how to balance and enhance your UQ potentials with the support of AI, maximizing opportunities and achieving exceptional results in all areas of your life. This exciting journey in pursuit of the maximum potential offered by the partnership between UQ and AI will allow you to uncover the secrets of this transformative collaboration and propel your success in all areas.

To consolidate our understanding, we revisited the importance of UQ balance as a metric and parameter to assess and develop human potentials. Based on scientific research and case studies, we saw how UQ goes beyond traditional metrics, incorporating essential potentials of 360-degree vision, resilience, adaptability, synchronicity, and emotional control.

We explored the application of UQ in leadership and building high-performance teams. We discussed strategies to develop synergy among team members and how UQ-parameterized AI can enhance team management, driving collective performance.

We also addressed the importance of adapting to market changes and how UQ can be a powerful tool in this process. We discussed the identification and anticipation of challenges in a VUCA environment, and how UQ-parameterized AI can drive smarter and more assertive business strategies.

Finally, we explored emerging trends and the evolution of UQ, along with the challenges and opportunities in adopting this approach in companies. We prepared ourselves for a UQ-oriented future, aware of the importance of keeping up with changes and preparing for the challenges that arise in this context.

As we conclude this journey, we invite you to be inspired and motivated to implement UQ in your company and personal life. We empower leaders and professionals to achieve exceptional results, transforming a conventional company into an intelligent one.

We stand at the dawn of a new era, where the balance of potentials and synchronous intelligence are key to business success. We hope this book has provided valuable insights, practical examples, and applicable strategies to propel your success and prepare you to face the challenges of the VUCA world.

Now is the time to embrace the transformative power of UQ and embark on a journey of personal and professional growth. This is just the beginning of a new era, where the balance of potentials and synchronous intelligence form the foundation for sustainable success.

We wish you continued success in your pursuit of UQ balance and that you achieve exceptional results in all areas of your life. Together, we can build a future driven by UQ, where human potential and AI merge harmoniously to achieve unprecedented success. Let's move forward toward this transformative journey and reach new levels of excellence.

Influences and References

Daniel Goleman - Author of the book "Emotional Intelligence" and one of the leading theorists of emotional intelligence. His research and insights on the importance of emotions in well-being and human success can provide a solid foundation for exploring the connection between UQ balance and emotional intelligence in the context of the business revolution.

Howard Gardner - Psychologist and author of the theory of multiple intelligences. His research on different forms of intelligence and the importance of valuing all human abilities and potentials can serve as a valuable reference for discussing UQ balance and comprehensive educational approaches in the context of the business revolution.

Carol Dweck - Psychologist and author of the book "Mindset: The New Psychology of Success." Her theory of growth mindset versus fixed mindset, which explores the belief that skills and intelligence can be developed through effort and continuous learning, can provide relevant insights into the importance of promoting holistic UQ development.

Clayton Christensen - Professor of Business Administration at Harvard and author of the book "The Innovator's Dilemma." His theory of disruptive innovation and the need for adaptability in a constantly changing world can contribute to the discussion on developing skills such as resilience and adaptability for UQ balance in the context of the business revolution.

Daniel Kahneman - Psychologist and author of the book "Thinking, Fast and Slow." His research on intuitive and analytical thinking can provide a basis for exploring the importance of critical thinking and informed decision-making for UQ balance.

Ray Kurzweil - Futurist and author of the book "The Singularity Is Near." His research and insights on technological advancement and the impact of artificial intelligence on the future of humanity can offer a comprehensive perspective on the potential of AI in various areas of life in the context of the business revolution.

Amy Cuddy - Social psychologist and author of the book "Presence: Bringing Your Boldest Self to Your Biggest Challenges." Her research on body language, confidence, and presence can be relevant to exploring how UQ balance can influence communication and interpersonal success.

Angela Duckworth - Psychologist and author of the book "Grit: The Power of Passion and Perseverance." Her research on the importance of perseverance and determination in achieving long-term goals can contribute to the discussion on resilience and human potential development in the context of AI utilization.

Michio Kaku - Theoretical physicist and author of the book "The Future of Humanity: Our Destiny in the Universe." His explorations of future technological possibilities, including AI, and their impact on the evolution of humanity can provide an inspiring and broad perspective on the use of AI in all areas of life in the context of the business revolution.

Sherry Turkle - Psychologist and author of the book "Alone Together: Why We Expect More from Technology and Less from

Each Other." Her research on the relationship between technology and human connection can be relevant for addressing the challenges and opportunities of balancing AI use with social and emotional interaction.

Biography of the Author

Katia Doria da Fonseca Vasconcelos is a writer and researcher with a background in Systems Analyst and extensive experience as a project leader in multinational and large-scale companies. Her professional journey has allowed her to understand the importance of balancing technological development with the human aspect for project success.

With a profound interest in understanding and dealing with human behavior in the organizational context, Katia focused her studies on Human Resources and the development of methodologies that promote synergy between technological needs and user expectations. Her experience as a project leader provided her with in-depth knowledge of how human emotions, thoughts, and behaviors directly influence the effectiveness of implemented systems.

As a writer and researcher, Katia shares her knowledge and experiences to inspire leaders and professionals to consider not only the technical aspects but also the human factor in project implementation and the development of effective solutions. Her integrative approach seeks to balance technological excellence with care for people, enabling systems to perfectly meet user demands and expectations.

In this book, Katia Doria da Fonseca Vasconcelos presents her unique and practical vision of the concept of UQ (Universal Synchronic Intelligence Quotient) and its application in the business context. Her UQ-based approach is grounded in her experience as a systems analyst and project leader, combining technical knowledge with an understanding of user needs and expectations.

Katia believes that the success of a project or a company is intrinsically linked to the ability to balance technological development with care for people. Her goal is to empower leaders and professionals to adopt a holistic approach that considers both technical and emotional dimensions, aiming to achieve exceptional results and fully satisfy user needs.

By sharing her knowledge and insights in this book, Katia Doria da Fonseca Vasconcelos invites readers to explore the transformative potential of UQ, integrating it into their leadership practices and project development. Her experience and expertise contribute to an expanded and updated view of the importance of balancing technology and the human aspect in the business context.

With a practical and inspiring approach, Katia seeks to provide readers with the necessary tools to tackle the challenges of the business world, considering the importance of balancing technical excellence with care for people. Her comprehensive and integrative vision allows leaders and professionals to build a path of sustainable success, aligning technological needs with user expectations and promoting a healthy and productive organizational culture.

Introducing the UQ series, a collection of books that explore the Universal Synchronic Intelligence Quotient (UQ) and its transformative impact in various areas of life. With a holistic and innovative approach, each book delves into different aspects of UQ, providing valuable insights and actionable practices to achieve success, balance, and fulfillment.

In "UQ in Creativity," discover how UQ can unlock your creativity and innovative potential, offering a fresh perspective to tackle creative challenges and find unique solutions.

In "UQ in the Digital Age," explore how UQ can help balance the use of technology with the need for human connection, well-being, and harmony in the ever-evolving digital era.

In the first edition of "UQ First Edition," delve into the

fundamentals of UQ, understanding its essence and practical application to achieve a holistic balance of mind, body, and soul.

"UQ The Principle of Human Evolution" explores how balancing UQ potentials and synchronicity can drive personal growth and development, leading you to new levels of self-discovery and evolution.

In "UQ in Project Management," discover how UQ can be applied to manage projects in a balanced and effective manner, optimizing resources, maximizing results, and successfully leading teams.

In the field of education, "UQ in Education" presents how UQ can enhance learning and prepare students for the future, promoting a holistic approach aligned with individual needs and potentials.

In the main book, "UQ Universal Synchronic Intelligence Quotient," explore the essence of UQ, learn to balance your potentials, and discover how to make the most of all areas of your life.

In "UQ The Power of UQ - The Theory of Balance," delve into the theory of UQ balance, offering profound insights into achieving a fulfilling and successful life by finding harmony between body, mind, and spirit.

"UQ in Health" explores how UQ can be applied to promote balanced health and holistic well-being, empowering you to achieve your best physical, mental, and emotional version.

Discover the intersection between UQ and artificial intelligence in "UQ in Artificial Intelligence," exploring how the combination of these two concepts can drive exceptional results in various areas.

In "UQ in Business Management," learn how to apply UQ to lead teams, make strategic decisions, and achieve exceptional results in the business world.

In "UQIAs and the New Reality of Remote work," discover how UQ and UQIAs tools can optimize productivity and well-being in the context of Remote work, balancing professional and personal demands.

Get moved by the "UQ Chronicles," an engaging series that tells stories filled with adventures, discoveries, and reflections on UQ and its impact on the lives of the characters.

Finally, "UQ The Power of UQ: The Theory of Balance" offers a profound insight into the theory of UQ balance, allowing you to find harmony and success in all areas of life.

Each book in the UQ series offers a unique and practical approach, combining scientific knowledge, case studies, and personal insights to empower you to achieve exceptional results and promote holistic balance in all areas of your life. Discover the transformative power of UQ and embark on a journey of personal growth and sustainable success.

All available on Amazon's KDP.